# THEY DIED TOO YOUNG

# AYRTON SENNA

BY

A. Noble

·PARRAGON·

This edition first published by Parragon Books Ltd in 1995

Produced by
Magpie Books Ltd, London

Copyright © Parragon Books Ltd 1995
Unit 13–17, Avonbridge Trading Estate
Atlantic Road, Avonmouth
Bristol, BS11 9QD

Illustrations courtesy of: Rex Features.

ISBN 0 75250 699 4

A copy of the British Library Cataloguing in Publication
Data is available from the British Library.

Typeset by Hewer Text Composition Services, Edinburgh
Printed in Singapore by Printlink International Co.

# THEY DIED TOO YOUNG
## Ayrton Senna

# Boy from Brazil

Ayrton Senna is up there with the immortals of motor racing, those men who, in their time, could drive like no one else, like Jim Clark, like Juan Fangio. There have been other great drivers, many of them, but these men could handle cars in a way beyond, where their vehicles became extensions of their bodies. They had nerves that went beyond those of other courageous drivers, a sort of controlled recklessness that was unbeatable. They also had that crucial ingredient, the will to win; the will to win is common among sportsmen, but in their cases it was incredibly intense, utterly obsessional. Absolutely nothing else mattered when they were out on the starting grid. There were no distractions, all that mattered was winning.

Ayrton Senna was born Ayrton Senna da Silva in São Paulo, Brazil, on 21 March 1960. Ayrton's father, Milton da Silva, ran a large car parts factory, employing over 700 workers, and owned several farms as well. So, at the least, Senna's family was well-to-do, if not multi-millionaire. A typically close South American family, it

provided Senna with a stable back-
ground, one to which he always
wanted to return. If home is where
the heart is, Senna's was always in Brazil.

At the age of four, his father made him
a 1-hp go-kart, which the tiny Senna
drove around in the garden and in the
parks of São Paolo. Apart from mark-
ing him out from most of the children
of São Paolo, who don't even have
shoes, it meant that his relationship
with the internal combustion engine
began extremely early. He also managed to drive one of his father's old farm
jeeps at a slightly later age, without
using the clutch which was too hard to
push. He could just tell from the tone
of the engine, and the whine of the
gearbox, when it was OK to change

gear. Apparently Jim Clark felt that his success had a lot to do with knowing machinery backwards at an early age, though in his case it was tractors. But the basics of a tractor or a jeep are the same as the basics of a racing car, and slithering round a farmyard is an excellent way of learning how tyre grip, chassis and power interact – just as advanced motorists learn to handle cars on skid pans.

By the age of ten, Senna had been given a more powerful go-kart. He wasn't allowed to race it until he was thirteen, so he practised at a course called Parque Anhembi. At thirteen he began to compete at the Interlagos track, where professional kart-racing took place. The racing gave him a taste for victory, as he kept on winning; one of his chief rivals was Maurizio Sala, who tried everything but could never get the edge. Apart from his driving skills, Senna generally had the best engine, as they were built for him by a specialist.

Go-karting is rough-and-tumble driving, with competitors pushing each other off the track, leaning wheel against wheel on those who present the greatest threat and mercilessly cutting up those who are too slow, diving in before corners, forcing them on to the less grippy mud and grass at the side of the track. It requires physical and mental toughness, vital training for any champion. Senna won the Brazilian Championship four times and in 1977, in the 100 cc international category won the South American Championship. He was a totally dedicated driver, not particularly friendly or talkative to his rivals. Winning was all, and he didn't want to risk losing by feeling any emotional attachment to the opposition.

When Senna was eighteen he headed off to Europe. Europe is at the heart of international motor racing, at all levels. There is some racing in the USA, such as Indy car racing, but it doesn't attract the worldwide following of the other racing circuses that tour globally but which do much of their actual racing in Europe. His first call was at the DAP kart factory in Milan, with whom he had booked a season's racing (at this

level, if he is not well known, the driver
pays to race). He tested karts for a while
at the international kart track at Parma,
where he showed a lot of raw ability if
little technique. Being able to go into
four-wheel slides and keep control may
have looked fancy, but it is not the
quickest way of getting round. It was
while on the karting circuit that Senna
met Mauricio and Stella Gugelmin who
became his closest friends in his long
self-imposed exile from Brazil. In those
early days Gugelmin helped Senna by
transporting Senna's kart in his sponsor's
lorry. In his first year, Senna came sixth
overall in the championships. He was
already using the technique he was
never to change – getting ahead of
the pack right at the beginning of a
race, when most drivers are still feeling

their way. This was new at the time, and the psychological advantage it gives the leader is crucial – don't wait for the tyres to warm up, just floor it. By the time the others have noticed what's happening it's too late.

He came back in 1979 for another shot at the title, but was unable to win. Due to inexperience, he and his mechanics would not use the practice sessions to the full, testing all the engines properly or preparing the karts to cope with changing track conditions. As soon as they found a fast set-up for the obtaining conditions that was it, even though the experienced teams could predict how the track would be later and would set up their karts accordingly. This meant that Senna might well have the fastest practice times, but was not among the leaders in the actual races. His urge to win, to be fastest all the time, was actually counterproductive, and it took him a while to learn that patience had a reward. His fearless style of driving also caused him a couple of accidents; he would always try to be right on the leader's tail and if anything sudden happened to the leader, as it did with Terry Fullerton, then world kart champion, who had an engine seizure, then Senna was in trouble, on this occasion being thrown out of his kart. In 1980 Senna had one last try at the kart championships at Nivelles in Belgium, but could only make second place.

Senna was now twenty. He was near the top of the karting world. He could either stay and hope to become champion or he could move on to higher things, Formula Ford 1600 and 2000, Formula 3, and, the ultimate, Formula 1. But his father wanted him to work in his factory, so Senna went to business college in São Paulo. The factory didn't work out, and Senna's father realized that only racing would make him happy. So in spring 1981, Senna returned to Europe, to Snetterton in Norfolk, in the hope of getting a Formula Ford 1600 drive for the season.

# Formula Ford

Senna settled in Norfolk, with his young wife, Liliane. He had arranged a season with the Van Diemen team, largely paid for by his father. There were three competitions open to him: the P & O, the Townsend Thoresen (TT) and the RAC. The racing would involve frequent visits to the same circuits, thereby giving drivers the opportunity to eliminate chance – they would all know the tracks and

Ayrton Senna

Senna took up go-kart racing at an early age

they were all driving the same 1600 cc cars. Senna was originally tried out in the 1980 model as there were no 1981s free and Van Diemen's Ralph Firmin didn't initially realize what a prodigy had arrived. As soon as he was behind the wheel, Firmin recognized that Senna had special talent – he wasn't just another rich would-be racer. Formula 1600 cars are quite different from karts: more powerful, but with much less grip, having high, narrow wheels. They are crude little machines, with clunky gearboxes, and despite the narrow tyres, it takes quite a lot of strength to steer them accurately with their tiny steering wheels.

On 1 March 1981 Senna competed in a round of the P & O Championship at

Brands Hatch. Senna was halfway up the grid when the race started, but managed to claw his way to fifth position by the end, eight seconds behind the winner, Argentinian Enrique Mansilla. Autosport commented: 'Undoubtedly we shall hear more of this young man.' Prophetic words. A week after this debut, Senna was at Thruxton for the first round of the TT Championship, where he duelled successfully with Mansilla, and came in third.

At Thruxton Senna met Keith Sutton, a photographer working for a Brazilian magazine. Senna saw Sutton as a means of publicizing himself; only a week later, at Brands Hatch again, in the second round of the TT Championship, in the wet, Senna stormed through to his first victory. Sutton was there to capture him on the top step of the rostrum. Senna and his wife were ecstatic. At Mallory Park, the following week, though, he was not so lucky – it was almost like the old karting days when, struggling to gain the lead from Mansilla, the latter forced him on to the grass and into second place. Senna was so incensed that after the race he actually physically attacked Mansilla, and the two had to be forcibly separated by the people around them.

At Snetterton, shortly afterwards, Senna's driving was witnessed by Dennis Rushen, who ran a 2000 Van Diemen team. It began to rain and all the drivers, except Senna, slowed down.

As he didn't come off, his lead grew unassailable. It took a sort of daredevil courage to risk this, together with the coolness to maintain precise control, a fairly unique combination. After the race Rushen offered Senna the British and European 2000 season for the bargain price of £10,000. Rushen was astonished at his skill in the wet. Senna went on in the season to win six races in a row – Donington, Brands Hatch, Oulton, Mallory Park, Brands Hatch again and Snetterton. At the last it rained, and while six cars spun off, Senna kept his nerve and his line. At the end of the race he had 105 points, Rick Morris 95 and Mansilla 75. In 1981, Senna won both the RAC and TT Championships.

Everybody thought that Ayrton would be back for 1982 in Formula 3, but much to everybody's surprise, he announced that he would be returning to Brazil to work with his father. The reason for this was that he had been unable to find a sponsor, despite his string of victories. Formula 1600 just didn't get the same coverage as the larger formulas, and no coverage, no sponsor. Another stab at the World Karting Championship at Parma came to nothing. The rules had changed to allow 135 cc engines, and Senna's kart frame was not strong enough for these. He only managed fourth. And he missed the Formula Ford Festival at Brands Hatch, which would have been a good opportunity to garner some publicity. His replacement in his vehicle, Tommy Byrne, did win it, so this was definitely an opportunity missed. An unhappy Senna returned to Brazil, fearing that his career could be over

# Formula 2000

From October 1981 to February 1982, Senna worked for his father's company. His father, initially opposed to his going back to racing, now changed his mind, and agreed to invest in Ayrton's career on the understanding that Ayrton would pay the investment back.

Senna returned at the beginning of the season. He didn't even bother to undergo extended practice sessions. He simply got straight into his car, received a brief lecture about slicks (smooth tyres used in the dry) and wings, which are there to keep the car firmly down on the tarmac, maximizing grip and acceleration. And, straightaway, he began winning, knocking the experts off their pedestals – Brands Hatch on 7 March, Oulton on the 27th, Silverstone on the 28th, and Donington on the 4 April, Snetterton on the 9th and Silverstone on the 12th. At Snetterton he had won despite losing his front brakes at an early stage. He slowed initially but as soon as he realized what had happened and had adjusted his driving style he simply pulled back into the lead. Because his

The young Senna with his father

Senna made it into Formula 1 in 1984

driving style was so consistent and controlled, Senna, unlike in his early days, could identify any problem with the components of his car, even down to which tyres had behaved in what way on a particular bend. This meant that his car could be set up to as near perfection as was humanly possible, which in turn helped him to get even further ahead.

Soon, the McLaren and Toleman teams approached him with a view to offering him a sponsored Formula 3 drive but amazingly Senna turned them down. It would have been an essential step, not just for the experience it would have given him, but because a new 'Superlicence' had been introduced for Formula 1, and one had to drive Formula 3 to get it. But Senna still wanted to shine in Formula 2000, where the playing field was more level. He felt he still had to learn the ropes, to complete his apprenticeship thoroughly, even if all his competitors were of the view that he was so outstanding he had little more to learn. But he wanted to be absolutely ready – he didn't want to drive Formula 1 until he was sure he would be champion. The offers flowed in: Williams and Lotus made approaches.

Senna went on to win the British and, then, the European 2000 Championship at Jyllandsring in Denmark. So in the first year, he had gone from unknown to double champion in Formula

2000. Apparently, on the last lap of the European, Senna admitted that he started to cry, he was so overwhelmed by his achievement. In the evening, he actually got drunk – normally he abstained – and joined in the general camaraderie, even going so far as to do 'wheelies' on a motorbike. Usually, he kept away from his fellow racers and teammates, presumably to maintain his phenomenal professional concentration; because of this some people saw him as unfriendly and stand-offish, though most of his closer friends say he in fact liked a joke and a laugh, but only when there was no job in hand.

Before 1982 was out, Senna had a last stab at the World Karting Championships in Kalmar, Sweden, but was dogged by bad luck and only came in fourteenth. This disappointment was enough for him to throw his last 2000 race at Brands Hatch. Out of his 28 races of the season this was one of only two he did not win, although he had to retire in four. He also had a single foray into Formula 3, courtesy of New Zealander Dick Bennetts, of West Surrey Racing (WSR). Mansilla had been driving for WSR and had a few wins: Senna didn't think much of Mansilla's skills, so he reasoned that if Mansilla could win with WSR then they must be providing a good car and this attracted him to the team. As he had now won the 2000 Championships he felt he could allow himself to graduate to Formula 3, and the race at Thruxton was to be televised, which was good for publicity. He was given Mansilla's car for the race, and as with all new vehicles, he was able to get the maximum out of it within minutes. He got pole position and won the race by 13 seconds, a commanding lead. Bennetts, not surprisingly, offered him a drive for 1983. The contract was signed in January 1983.

# Formula 3

Formula 3 is challenging. The twenty rounds of the 1983 Marlboro Formula 3 Championship were to take place from March to October, which means one has the full variety of English weather to contend with. Six circuits were to be used. The first race was to be at Silverstone on 6 March, to which WSR was sending Senna in a Ralt-Toyota. Another Ralt-Toyota, prepared by Eddie Jordan Racing, was

Senna flies by at the 1990 French Grand Prix

Senna takes time out to fly a Mirage

also appearing, to be driven by another ambitious hopeful, Martin Brundle. Brundle was aware that Senna was a real threat; his reputation had preceded him, even though, apart from the one drive the previous year, Senna had no F3 experience. At Silverstone, a driver called Leslie Dennis took pole, which was something of an upset, as in previous testing Senna and Brundle had both been on the lap record, set only the previous year. Senna was soon past Dennis and won with a 7-second lead over Brundle.

At Thruxton in the wet Senna won again; it seemed odd that Brundle was quicker down the straights than Senna, but it turned out that Senna's engine wouldn't go over 5,600 rpm (when it should have reached at least 7,000) which meant he suffered from a severe power disadvantage. He pulled himself into the lead, though, by being quicker on the corners. At Silverstone a week later, he was beaten off the start by Brundle, but managed to overtake him on the outside, with two wheels on the grass, an almost unbelievable feat. The string of successes continued and in May Senna beat the world record of eight successive wins, set by Nelson Piquet in 1978, with nine. The tactic of starting a race as quickly as possible, without waiting to settle down into a car, threw the other drivers. While they were still struggling to get their concentration up to speed, so to speak, they suddenly found that this was a luxury they could not afford; the pack could no longer move off almost as one to sort itself out over the race, because, immediately, one member of the pack had already left it behind. Instead of being able to build up a challenge over time, shaving off a second here, a second there, they had to reach the peak of speed and concentration instantaneously. This gave Senna a huge advantage. He went on to take a tenth successive victory, beating Brundle by 10 seconds at Silverstone on 30 May. Williams approached Senna for a test Formula 1 run.

Two weeks later, the almost unthinkable happened. Brundle switched from British to European tyres, which gave him a little extra speed. The points from this race could be put towards either the British or the European Championship. With this edge Brundle got pole position, and then when the race started he did a Senna, roaring off into the distance. Senna had to struggle to hold off the third runner, Johnny Dumfries. Senna, too, had played around with his tyres, running three different types in the hope that they would last the race. His left rear tyre apparently lost grip, and eventually he spun off on the chicane. Brundle knew he was going to win, and did.

This failure led Senna to make several mistakes in ensuing races, he so hated being second. At Cadwell Park on 19 June he ran into a marshal's post, wrecking his car and putting himself

out of the race. At Snetterton on 3 July
he rode up and over Brundle's rear
wheel, spinning off and putting himself out of the race. Bennetts had to
talk to him to try to get him to accept
second place on occasion – otherwise
his points lead could be seriously
threatened. Senna won his next at
Silverstone on 16 July but at Donington on the 24th, he was actually beaten
by Brundle in a completed race. At
Oulton, the next race, Senna was so
desperate to beat Brundle that in a
risky slide manoeuvre he managed to
put both Brundle and himself out of
the race, for which he was fined and
had his licence endorsed. The rest of
the season, until the last three races,
was peppered with pointless accidents;
the Championship was in the bag for

Senna if he could bear to come in
second, and there was no need at all
to come in first. By 2 October Brundle
actually overtook Senna in points, 123
to 122. There were only two races left,
the Macau Grand Prix and Thruxton.
At Macau, Senna managed to get pole
at position and fastest lap, despite
damaging the wheels but not the
chassis of his car against a wall on
the winding Monaco-like circuit. It
was his first street race and he won.
Thruxton would decide the British
Championship. There was some tension, including a desperate race for
technical advantage. Jordan's Nova-
motor engine had some factory mod-
ifications that WSR's didn't, but WSR
had managed to wheedle 1984 side-
pods from Ralt, which improved the

aerodynamics of his car. Senna also had taped up his oil radiator outlet, so that his engine would warm up more quickly. When the race began he hared off into the distance, but at lap 6 he had to remove the tape which required unbuckling himself and leaning forward to take off the tape – he did so just at the approach to the chicane, and for an instant thought the race might be over for him, but luckily he managed to get back properly into his seat in time, and that was it. He was even able to slow down a little by the end as the chequered flag came down.

In the meantime, he had tested a Marlboro McLaren, with Brundle and Stefan Bellof, another promising young driver. He was witnessed by Herbie Blash, Brabham's team manager, who wanted to offer him a drive. Before the year was out he tested for Toleman, whose designer, Rory Byrne, was immediately impressed. He wanted him.

# Formula 1

Toleman had only made it from Formula 2 into Formula 1 in 1981, getting their first points in 1983. But in 1983, their driver Derek Warwick was offered a drive with Renault, which he took, as he thought they would give him his best shot at the World Championship. Senna was to be his replacement. They would have taken Brundle, but Alex Hawkridge, Toleman's manager, preferred Senna, simply because of his success in Formula 3. Brabham also wanted Senna, but Nelson Piquet said no, and as one of Brabham's sponsors, Parmalat, were connected with Piquet, that was it. Lotus had been interested in Senna too, but felt that they had to keep a British driver, one Nigel Mansell, to keep John Player, a British company and a valuable sponsor, happy.

Senna signed an unusual contract, which stated that he could leave Toleman if the car wasn't good enough. He would have to pay for this privilege and give notice before moving on, but the contract offered an escape route if need be.

At the start of the season, the Tolemans were seriously uncompetitive.

Senna celebrates one of his many victories

Nigel Mansell and Nelson Piquet

The main reason for this was that their tyres, Pirellis, were not as good as the competition's. Basically, the big teams (Brabham, McLaren, Lotus, Ligier, Ferrari, Tyrell, Williams) ran on Michelins and Goodyears, and the small teams were left with Pirellis. Hawkridge approached Michelin and was allowed to use their previous year's tyres, obviously not as good as 1984's. McLaren had some agreement with Michelin that stopped smaller teams from competing with the latest rubber. At Imola things came to a head, when Toleman did not participate in the first day's qualifying session; they didn't want to get into a row with Pirelli on the latter's home ground. The next day, Saturday, Senna failed to qualify due to a fuel-pressure

problem and Toleman were no longer in the race. The following Monday,
Hawkridge and Senna went off to
Dijon to test the new season's car,
the TG 184, on year-old Michelins.
The difference in performance was
staggering, and the Toleman team's
morale soared.

The first real test came at the Monaco
Grand Prix. Not only is the track
fiendishly difficult to negotiate, it is
also impossible to overtake for most of
it. On the day, 3 June 1984, it
bucketed with rain, magnifying the
drivers' difficulties immensely. Luckily for Toleman, Michelin could not
send Senna out on slicks, and they
only had the latest sort of rain tyres,
so Toleman would be running the

same rubber as McLaren. The race was epic. Mansell crashed, having held the lead for a short period, while Senna doggedly pushed his way up the ranking. Ninth on the first lap, sixth by lap 10, fourth in lap 14, third in lap 16, and by the end of lap 19, only Alain Prost was still in front – 33.841 seconds in front. Lap by lap, apart from the 21st, Senna whittled away at those seconds. By lap 31, there were only 7.5 seconds between them. But Prost had been signalling for the race to stop, and Jackie Ickx, the official starter, brought the race to an end. As Prost slowed towards the end of 32, Senna zipped past him. He thought he'd won. Unfortunately, the positions were decided on the basis of lap 31. Many thought Senna had been robbed – the race should have been 78 laps long and the consensus was that he had Prost's measure. There were mutterings about the Grand Prix establishment having fixed things in McLaren's favour.

Having made his mark, Senna's next few races in North America were a disappointment. Mechanical failure and track failure (at Dallas) kept Toleman down the running order. Senna's sole venture into the World Sportscar Championships at the Nürburgring in a Porsche 956 with Henri Pescarolo and Stefan Johansson was not a great success either. Rain affected the electronics and the car had a puncture and clutch trouble. None the less the team came in

Senna at the controls of his McLaren

Living it up at the Rio carnival

eighth, and all were impressed by Senna's uncanny ability to switch to a totally different machine, successfully and without hesitation. Back on the GP circuit Senna managed a third at Brands Hatch on 22 July, but thereafter there was a series of disappointing runs with mechanical failures ruining his chances. Also Michelin announced they were withdrawing from racing. Toleman had already annoyed Goodyear in Formula 2, and had fallen out with Pirelli. The future looked bleak. It was the end for Toleman as far as Senna was concerned.

At Zandvoort in August a bombshell landed in the Toleman camp. While they were entertaining potential sponsors in their motorhome, two journalists arrived and told them that Senna had signed for Lotus. It was a cruel blow for Toleman, to hear that they were losing their best driver in these circumstances, and it didn't impress the sponsors much either. Hawkridge responded by dropping Senna at Monza. This was the most appropriate punishment in his eyes, as Senna's greatest joy in life was testing himself to the limit in a race. Johansson replaced him and came fourth, so they knew that the car wasn't that bad, especially as it was still running on year-old tyres. But Senna's mind was made up – Lotus offered him an opportunity to win the World Championship, whereas Toleman didn't.

# Lotus

Once in at Lotus, for the 1985 season, Senna immediately made an impact. His teammate was Elio de Angelis, who had been with Lotus since 1980. When Senna arrived he somehow became the focus of the team, despite de Angelis's seniority. His first race was in Brazil. He immediately established himself in qualifying, being placed on the second row, and was in third position at lap 48 before his electrics gave up. Estoril in

Portugal was his next stop. Here he showed his calibre, lapping in the qualifying session at 1 minute 21.007 seconds. In the race itself it rained and Senna did temporarily lose control. But out of twenty-six runners only ten were still there at the end of the race – and not only was he one of them, he was first. It was his first Grand Prix win. Amazingly, he was quite calm about it: Peter Warr, Lotus's manager, was ecstatic.

For the rest of the season, apart from hiccups at Imola, Montreal and Silverstone, Senna was always up with the leaders, except when mechanical trouble forced him out. What he had was a quality of consistency that other drivers were simply staggered by, not just because he could follow the right line

43

so closely but that he could do it lap
after lap. The intensity of his dedication was of a different order from that
of his rivals. It was one of the reasons,
some speculate, that he and his wife
divorced after only a year of marriage,
and that he did not seem to get close to
many people. He simply had room in
his mind for only one thing, and at that
he was consummate. One commenta-
tor even joked that for Senna Bo
Derek was a Ferrari. At the end of
the season, Senna was in fourth place,
with 38 points. Teammate de Angelis
had only 33, and left for Brabham.

Lotus needed to replace de Angelis,
and Derek Warwick was free as Renault had withdrawn from F1. But
Senna didn't want Warwick, and this

led to bad blood between the two drivers and between Senna and the British motoring press. But in this opinion he was perfectly logical, given that he thought that Lotus was in too weak a state to field two top-class drivers. Johnny Dumfries was his preferred choice. Lotus soon found out that Senna dominated the workshop and the pits. He had always had a phenomenal ability to size up a car and the way it was set up, as Toleman and others had already found out. Everything had to be perfect, and if it was not, it had to be done again. On the track, he would memorize every bump and wrinkle and could describe his performance lap by lap afterwards. He also talked to everybody concerned, storing up the information in

Senna's rival Alain Prost

At the start of the 1992 Grand Prix at Imola

his excellent memory, so that he would be able to milk every last drop of performance out of his car.

He was moving into the record books; in 1985 he had pole position seven times. The record, held by Lauda (1974) and Piquet (1984) was nine. He was already at Jim Clark's 1963 total. In the first race of 1986, the Brazilian GP, he had pole and came second in the race. In the Spanish GP at Jerez, he had pole and victory. In his next eight races, those that he completed, he was never below fifth and he was pole eight times. Mechanical trouble forced him out of several races: Imola, Brands Hatch, Osterreichring, Monza, Adelaide. Though with some generosity of spirit, when he spun off in the French GP he actually apologized to the mechanics – he, not the machine, had failed them. At the end of the season he was fourth again, but with 55 points, over 50 per cent more than the previous year.

1987 was Senna's third season with Lotus and this would be the make-or-break of his relationship with them. From his point of view, they had to be able to supply him with a car that could win the World Championship. They had a new engine supplier, Honda, as Renault was pulling out of F1. There is some debate as to whether the Renault engines were better than the Hondas. Senna always got poor fuel consumption out of them – a critical factor, as one obviously wants to keep

refuelling time to the absolute mini-
mum. He also got the worst fuel
performance from the Hondas, out of
four drivers. This was partly because he
was the fastest, simply burning up more
fuel, but also perhaps because he was
constantly near full power so as to make
up for a deficient chassis.

The first race of the season, Brazil, was
not a great success. Lotus had a new
'active' suspension, where the suspension 'predicts' to some extent how the
wheels should move as soon as it senses
a bump. Senna moved up and down
the order like a yo-yo. At Imola he
simply could not outpace Mansell in a
Williams, despite getting pole. At Spa
the two duelled again, until on a corner
their wheels brushed against each

other, the two cars locked together, and both spun off. Senna was in a sand pit, while Mansell managed to get back on the track and as far as lap 17 before giving up. He then went into the Lotus pit and grabbed Senna by the throat. It took three Lotus mechanics to get Mansell off Senna. Emotions run high on the race track, the minute pure concentration takes a rest.

As the season ran on, Senna avoided repeating this incident, and began racing in a way that would accumulate points – if there was a problem with the car, tyres, fuel consumption, whatever, he would moderate his driving so as to get a place, rather than risk all to come in first. This strategy paid off as by the seventh

GP of the season, Silverstone, he led by 31 points to Mansell's and Piquet's 30, and Prost's 26, having achieved a the following placings in the previous five races: 2nd, 1st, 1st, 4th, 3rd. At Hockenheim, the next race, at the end of July, Senna had a dangerous tyre deflation in practice. Whether it was this that made up his mind for him or not, he decided that Lotus were not going to bring him the Championship. He had discussions with Ron Dennis of McLaren, and his lawyers wrote to Warr to tell him that Senna would not be with Lotus the following year. Warr acted fast and signed up Piquet for 1988, even before Senna had physically signed with McLaren. Senna heard about Piquet's signing two days after the event, which clearly irritated him; it was a reminder that he was not indispensable, that his departure would not throw his team into a state of shock. As the season went on, Senna fell down the order, as Piquet asserted his dominance. Any hope of staying near Piquet disappeared in Mexico on 18 October when he spun off. At Adelaide, the last race of the season, he was second but disqualified due to technical irregularities with the car. It was all something of an anticlimax. But he had come a creditable third, and he and Lotus retained good feelings about each other. He had given them the sort of focus and involvement that helps a team towards success, and they had worked hard to give him a competitive car.

Senna in his private plane

Senna with Frank Williams and Damon Hill

# The Champion

Senna's first job with McLaren was to test the new MP4/4 car: a brand new car, with a Honda engine, the first Honda that McLaren had run. Testing was at Imola, and Prost, Senna's team-mate, was first at the wheel. His time was 1 minute 28.5. Senna then had a trial and shaved 0.9 of a second off. The design chief, Steve Nichols, was well pleased. This was two seconds faster than the new Ferrari had managed.

The season kicked off at Rio de Janeiro on 3 April 1988. Senna had pole. But at the start, he had a gearbox problem and another car caught fire. The first start was abandoned. Senna went into the pits to change cars. This cost him time, but slowly he hauled himself up the running order, till he was second at lap 20. Then a bodged pit stop lost him half a minute. He was now sixth. But out he went again, until lap 31, when he was disqualified – it was against the rules to change cars after the official start, and that was the abandoned one.

Imola made up for this disappointment, Senna coming in a clear first from Prost, just making it with an almost empty tank. Monaco was a revelation as Senna

claimed pole and set the fastest lap; Prost
was the only person near him. But
during the race Senna momentarily
lost concentration and hit the barrier.
He was out of it. This momentary lapse
reminded him of his human frailty – the
one reason he had *not* lost races was
through loss of concentration. Prost
won at Monaco as he did in Mexico,
12 days later, with Senna behind him.
At Montreal the two McLarens paced
each other, in front of the pack, with
Senna making his winning bid on lap
19. Detroit on 19 June, no argument;
Senna led all the way, despite problems
with the track condition.

For the French GP it was the McLarens again, this time Prost from
Senna. It was starting to look like a

one-team Championship. Practice at
Silverstone brought some surprises
though. Senna spun the car twice,
and Michele Alboreto and Gerhard
Berger knocked the McLarens off
pole. It poured on the day, 10
July, which was bad news for McLaren. Wet-weather tyres increase fuel
consumption, and with the McLarens this had been something of a
problem. It's dangerous racing in the
rain, and Prost and Senna almost
knocked each other out; Berger led
till lap 14 when Senna slipped past
him, while Prost retired with mechanical problems. But Senna did
not let go, and McLaren clocked
up their eighth successive win of
the season.

Flowers at the barrier where Ayrton Senna died

A fan mourns at Ayrton Senna's funeral

After this the tension really built up: the points accumulated over the season meant that Senna had moved from third to second at Montreal, creeping up on Prost, until after the Hungaroring on 7 August the two men were level at 66 points each. Senna had now won six times, equalling Jim Clark's 1963 and Prost's own 1984 season records. The third runner, Berger, was nowhere in sight with 28 points. Spa on 26 August; a clean lead by Senna from start to finish. His great goal was now in sight, with a three-point lead. There were five races left. At Monza, Senna got pole, his ninth in a season, gaining a new record. Prost pushed Senna hard, even though he had a technical malfunction that caused him to drop out on lap 35.

The Ferraris took over the chase, so Senna could not relax, and then suddenly a Williams was out of control in front of him in the chicane. Disaster, as the two cars contacted. Senna was out of the race. At Estoril on 25 September Prost and Senna duelled manically, Senna nearly forcing Prost into the pit-lane wall. Prost won, as Senna dropped back to sixth. Afterwards there was real anger between the two men, and they ceased to act as a team. Prost was now five points ahead of Senna, with 81. After Jerez, Prost stayed on top, with 84 to Senna's 79. There were only two races left in the season, Suzuka and Adelaide. But because the World Championship is decided on one's eleven best finishes, Senna was by no means out of it.

Meanwhile, now that the competition between the McLaren drivers was less than friendly, there was a suggestion from FIA, the sport's governing body, that Honda might not treat the two drivers absolutely equally. Honda, now the manufacturers' World Champion, refuted this suggestion with extreme courtesy. There was no question but that Honda would observe the rules of fair play.

Suzuka: Senna's twelfth pole of the season, waiting for the red, then the green light. He stalled, the cars behind streaming past him. Luckily, oh so luckily, the starting grid at Suzuka is on a slope. The McLaren rolled forward, the engine caught, and then died again. Another try, and mercifully it caught. But Senna was fourteenth, while Prost and Berger fought it out in the far distance, building up a lead between themselves and the pack. By the end of lap 1, Senna had moved to eighth, in lap 2 he made sixth, but there were still 9 long clear seconds between him and Prost. The gap actually expanded to 13 seconds by lap 4, and stayed there for the fifth. But then Senna got his pace and had cut off a second by the tenth lap. Ivan Capelli in a March was jousting now with Prost and actually drew level with him in lap 15. Light rain had begun to fall, and rain was Senna's element. Capelli dropped out with a failed engine, and now there was nobody between Senna and Prost, and at last Senna could actually see his target.

The rain was getting worse, and finally in lap 27 Senna roared past Prost on a straight. The lead was his, never to be lost. He had made it. He was World Champion. Adelaide didn't matter. Second was good enough. A great year, 13 pole positions, eight outright victories.

## 1989 – 94

The new season started amicably enough for McLaren at Rio, but at Imola the latent animosity between Prost and Senna burst out. Senna won, but in so doing he had overtaken Prost on the approach to a bend. Senna would argue that he had done so on a straight, but Prost said it was on the bend itself. Why he became so angry about it was because in the previous year, the two drivers had reached an informal agreement not to overtake each other when braking into a bend. Prost described Senna as dishonest in an interview with *L'Equipe* magazine. The McLaren manager tried to smooth things over, but it was too late. The drivers were no longer on speaking terms, and simply got on hard-headedly with their jobs. Senna went on to win Monaco and the Mexican Grand Prix. In Phoenix for the American GP, he topped Jim Clark's record 33 pole positions. But at Phoenix and in the next three races he was dogged by mechanical problems and had to retire in all. Hockenheim was his next victory, when Prost lost a gear with three laps left. Senna was second to Mansell at the Hungaroring, and first again at Spa, before having to retire in the next two races. Prost began complaining again at Monza that McLaren was not treating the two drivers equally. Prost agreed to drive for Ferrari the following year. McLaren and Honda, of course, denied any favouritism, but it was too late.

More bad blood was to flow in Grands Prix that year. In the Portuguese GP Mansell was disqualified for reversing in the pits, but did not retire. On the 49th lap, his and Senna's car collided on a bend, and that was the end of the race for Senna. There was an argument afterwards over whether Mansell had seen the black flag ordering him to retire on lap 39, and tempers grew heated. Ferrari and its driver were fined $50,000 with Mansell banned from the Spanish Grand Prix. Ironically Senna missed a black flag at Jerez, which he proceeded to win after incurring a fine of $20,000. At Suzuka, Prost was determined to give Senna a real race, and so he did, until lap 47, when the two drivers became entangled and slid off together. Senna managed to get going again, but had to come in for a new nose. He ended the race in the lead but was disqualified. McLaren appealed, more in an attempt to clear the air than anything else; after all, this race would decide which of their two drivers was World Champion. All Senna's past mishaps and risky manoeuvres were dragged up and he received a $100,000 fine and a six-month suspension. McLaren and he were crestfallen, the stuffing knocked out of them. After a delay, in which the racing world wondered whether Senna or McLaren would pay the fine and get a new licence for the 1990 season, McLaren paid the fine.

The 1990 season started at Phoenix, where Senna won as though on automatic pilot. In Brazil something of the old spark came back, as he felt he was racing for the nation. Gradually the old confidence and awareness returned. Because of a shunt he was only third, but he seemed mentally back up to scratch. In Hungary though his concentration lapsed slightly and he drove Nannini, ahead of him, out of the race, coming in third himself. At Spa, he and Prost had a press-conference reconciliation. It was as if these men of determination and dedication were beginning to recognize that there were things that mattered outside racing. Qualifying for the Spanish Grand Prix, a Lotus driver, Martin Donnelly, had a bad accident. Senna went to visit the wreckage and, later, Donnelly in hospital. Senna also began to express a concern for the poor of his homeland in his later years.

The season continued with Senna establishing a clear lead until the last two races, Suzuka and Adelaide. Senna was on his 51st pole at Suzuka. The race started, and ten seconds later it was over, as far as Senna and Prost were concerned. It was almost a rerun of 1989, with the Championship positions reversed. Prost was furious and claimed that Senna had simply pushed him off the track. Senna simply stated that if pole position had been switched to the other side of the track, as he had requested, the accident would never have happened. Ferrari threatened to leave Formula 1 altogether if, as they saw it, this sort of tactic was becoming accepted. A special safety commission was set up by FIA to assess the tactics of drivers in the 1990 season, with effects on their licences for 1991. The season ended, as usual, at Adelaide, where Senna hit a barrier. It didn't matter, he was Champion again.

During 1991 Senna seemed less hectic, not always pushing so near and, sometimes, beyond the limit, as he had done

in the past. He was prepared to accumulate points without expecting to
dominate every race. But seven wins
were enough to beat off the Mansell
challenge and he had his third Championship. It was to be his last. And at
Suzuka, some of the new calmer Senna
seemed to have disappeared, as he
brought up the problems of the previous year in a scathing attack on the
recently departed president of FIA.

1992 was a miserable season, with the
McLaren hopelessly outclassed by the
new Williams–Renaults of Mansell
and Riccardo Patrese. At the end of
the year Senna was fourth, behind
Mansell (108 pts), Patrese (56) and
Michael Schumacher (53). 1993 was
even worse. Honda withdrew from

F1, and McLaren had to make do with a Ford engine, which was far worse than both the Williams and the Benetton Fords, which had priority with Ford. Senna had hoped to drive for Williams but they took on Prost, as Mansell had left after not receiving the required salary. A clause of Prost's contract, not unnaturally, stipulated that Williams were not to take on Senna. Senna had even offered to drive for Williams unpaid, which is a measure of how desperate he was about the 1993 season. Senna did manage some successes against all the odds, at Donington and Monaco, and finished the season on a high, first in both the Japanese and the Australian GPs. He came in a creditable second behind Prost in the Championship. At the end of the year Prost announced his retirement, and the way opened for Senna to move to Williams, whose car he had test driven so many years earlier.

# The Last Lap

1994 must have looked good to Senna. Each time he had changed team his talents had developed, and the number of his successes had increased. It started well enough in the first three races – pole each time; Brazil, the Pacific GP and the San Marino GP at Imola. But at Interlagos he spun off, and in the second race he was knocked off by his replacement at McLaren, Mika Hakkinen.

Imola, 29 April 1994. Death and ill-fortune hung over the race. In practice, Sasol Jordan driver Rubens Barrichello crashed badly, but got away with a broken nose and some bruised ribs. Senna visited Barrichello in hospital. He had predicted at the beginning of the year that removal of the electronics from the cars – the traction control, the anti-lock braking and the 'active' suspension – would lead to more accidents. The FIA had changed the rules because these devices gave the richer teams, who could afford them, too much of an advantage. The rule change would make racing more competitive, but they did not consider the human cost.

On the Saturday, Roland Ratzenberger, a popular figure in his first F1 season, also crashed. He was not so lucky as Barrichello and died shortly afterwards. Senna drove to the scene of the accident to see what had happened, even though race officials tried to stop him. He was deeply affected by this tragedy and did not take part in the practice session that day. When he phoned his fiancée, Adrienne Galitseu, whom he had met a year earlier, he told her that he did not want to race the following day. He talked with Niki Lauda about safety. Senna, Berger and Schumacher had agreed that something should be done about driver safety, and a drivers' meeting was planned in Monaco for eleven days after Imola.

Imola, 1 May 1994, the race itself. There was a crash as the race began, and it had to be restarted when the wreckage was cleared away. Senna led the pack, with Schumacher on his tail. And then, on lap 7, at over 190 mph, Senna reached the Tamburello corner, which is really a kink between two straights. But Senna did not take the bend, he just went straight on, over a run-off area, and hard into a concrete wall, at over 160 mph. The car was demolished, Senna slumped in the cockpit. A helicopter flew him the 25 miles to the Maggiore hospital. He was in a coma – his heart had to be restarted by the medical team at the site of the crash – but his forehead was crushed beyond medical skill. Brain death

hands before the race and Prost had said maybe they might be friends again in the future. It was not to be.

had happened at the wall. Life ceased at 6.40 pm.

In Brazil, three days of national mourning were declared. The May Day mass in Rio was dedicated to Ayrton Senna. Weeping crowds gathered outside his parents' home, and outside his apartment. He was the greatest Brazilian sports hero since Pélé, and now he was gone. President Itmar Franco offered the presidential aircraft to fly his body back home. At Williams's headquarters in Didcot, Oxfordshire, well-wishers paid their respects with flowers. At the funeral, on 5 May, the crowds in São Paolo were immense. Alain Prost was one of the pallbearers. Senna and Prost had shaken